THE AMERICAN POETRY REVIEW/

The Honickman Foundation is dedicated to the support of projects that p___ spiritual growth and creativity, education, and social change. At the heart of the mission of the Honickman Foundation is the belief that creativity enriches contemporary society because the arts are powerful tools for enlightenment, equity, and empowerment, and must be encouraged to effect social change as well as personal growth. A current focus is on the power of photography and poetry to reflect and interpret reality, and hence, to illuminate all that is true.

The annual American Poetry Review/Honickman First Book Prize offers publication of a book of poems, a $3,000 award, and distribution by Copper Canyon Press through Consortium. Each year a distinguished poet is chosen to judge the prize and write an introduction to the winning book. The purpose of the prize is to encourage excellence in poetry and to provide a wide readership for a deserving first book of poems. *Vantage* is the twenty-second book in the series.

WINNERS OF THE AMERICAN POETRY REVIEW / HONICKMAN FIRST BOOK PRIZE

1998 Joshua Beckman, *Things Are Happening*

1999 Dana Levin, *In the Surgical Theatre*

2000 Anne Marie Macari, *Ivory Cradle*

2001 Ed Pavlić, *Paraph of Bone & Other Kinds of Blue*

2002 Kathleen Ossip, *The Search Engine*

2003 James McCorkle, *Evidences*

2004 Kevin Ducey, *Rhinoceros*

2005 Geoff Bouvier, *Living Room*

2006 David Roderick, *Blue Colonial*

2007 Gregory Pardlo, *Totem*

2008 Matthew Dickman, *All-American Poem*

2009 Laura McKee, *Uttermost Paradise Place*

2010 Melissa Stein, *Rough Honey*

2011 Nathaniel Perry, *Nine Acres*

2012 Tomás Q. Morín, *A Larger Country*

2013 Maria Hummel, *House & Fire*

2014 Katherine Bode-Lang, *The Reformation*

2015 Alicia Jo Rabins, *Divinity School*

2016 Heather Tone, *Likenesses*

2017 Tyree Daye, *River Hymns*

2018 Jacob Saenz, *Throwing the Crown*

2019 Taneum Bambrick, *Vantage*

VANTAGE

VANTAGE

Taneum Bambrick

The American Poetry Review
Philadelphia

Cover photo: Matthew Genitempo
Book design and composition: Gopa & Ted2, Inc.
Distribution by Copper Canyon Press / Consortium

Library of Congress Control Number: 2019930307

ISBN 978-0-9833008-8-5 cloth
ISBN 978-0-9860938-0-7 paper

9 8 7 6 5 4 3

For my parents

CONTENTS

INTRODUCTION BY SHARON OLDS

Vantage is a moving, radical work of art, written in a quiet, clear voice. Taneum Bambrick has given us an extraordinary first book. Part of its freight has to do with ecological devastation, told with no voluptuous sentiment. Not "told" so much as seen—the ferocious images not metaphor but reality. Not ideas but things.

These are poems of daring clarity, of uneasy beauty and terror, without pretension or drama. The poems' deft lines, their elegant ordinary absence of high tone—their music in the presence of their horrific content—present a picture of the current state in our progress toward the end of the world as we know it.

And *Vantage* is a deep pleasure to read. Our guide does not draw attention to our guide. The surreal narrative is rich with nonpersonal intimacy: intimacy with refuse, with the trashed earth; with work, with eros, with fellow-workers, with family; with mortality—and it is strong with a lack of self-interest or self-indulgence.

Many characters emerge, in the story of the town of Vantage, which has been drowned by a dam: the recreational grounds and killing fields up at the surface above the water; rivers, soil, jet-skis, snakes, garbage, pollutants, sacrificed animals. The voice—which calls itself *I*, or *you*, or *we*—is capable, humble, accurate, illuminating (with no extra sparkle). It presents for our eyes and noses, hands, ears, brains (sight, smell, touch, hearing, thinking, dreaming, nightmaring) what many of us have not yet seen—the toxic dump the earth is becoming—and what the youngest of us will be required eventually to make a home in.

The speaker's voice is at home in several crafts: prose-poem; lyric; essay-poem; stretched lyric (with a lot of space and time—a lot of paper—showing through); off-rhyme, off-rhythm, off-image; impeccable off-grammar.

Partway through, the book includes in its subject the luxury of the teller's privilege in terms of class—there is a moral alertness in the telling. The book embodies a vision in which fact is as unsettling as the weirdest, most powerful metaphor.

There is very little figurative language in *Vantage*. The images themselves (some gleaned as a member of a river and dam clean-up crew) function as metaphors.

In another sense, something like metaphor is ever-present in the poems, as if, alongside the environmental wreckage, is the planet when only the First People were here. What we have done and are doing to the globe and to its species (and to each other) is as wild as an image of hell. (Dead rivers and creatures stand also as metaphors for the condition of our souls as dwellers and caretakers.)

Vantage gives us a landscape of fatal truth, difficult honesty, irony, self-pitilessness, and respect for community. The poems do not glance over but sing—strictly, and with a haunting physicality—in the presence of sexism, addiction, classism, racism, genderism, family, and sexuality.

The relative absence of figurative language also means that, vivid as *Vantage* is—for the senses and the imagination—it does not underline the import of anything by drawing us away from matter to spirit. Matter, in relation to the land we inhabit, *is* spirit. As Forrest Gander wrote, in *Redstart*, "Poetry doesn't simply supplement the rational intellect but provides inherent and sometimes incommensurable forms of insight. Because its meanings are neither quantitative nor verifiable, poetry may offer different, subtler, and more complex expressions than the language of information and commerce. An ecological poetry might even . . ." (I love that ellipsis, as if we fear to voice our wisp of hope for the earth.)

Vantage is a work of art which also functions as a call, as if from under the ground, a cry from water and air. By means of common, startling, original sense-perception, our imagination of the present and future is awakened. Taneum Bambrick's art emcompasses this without polemic. By raising up, before our inner eyes, the presence of today's increasing damage, the book helps us to believe in the disaster we are in—and to understand that each of us, as well as each leader, is responsible. It's as if, if we imagine the death of this planet as we know it, we might work harder to attempt to delay that death.

Finally, *Vantage* is a love poem to the creature which is the earth, to its substance and flora and fauna, including us: imperfect as each of us is in our ability to love; and loved as each of us could be. I love this essential, gorgeous work of art, and thank Taneum Bambrick for it.

Sharon Olds
January, 2019

LITTER

I become a part of this garbage crew
empty cans along
the Wanapum pool.
Peel condoms off rock
beside fire pits—
call them *snakeskins*.
I learn quick.
When there's a hoof
in the road I know
to grope through the ditch
for the rest of the goat.
Sling bags so they won't split,
my uniform juiced with intestines
of liquefied King Salmon.
I shovel a pit bull
from a plastic tub
in a parking lot—he's dense
and flat at the belly,
a figurine.
I stop dry heaving
over the dead-animal-dumpster
at headquarters, even as it vibrates
with maggots, the stink
generating its own heat.
And as the torso
of a man is fished from the river
I wade in to my knees.
Watching for bones, coils
of skin, I try to imagine
his knife-bisection
at the hips, the sound
of a spine snapped.
My litter grabbers outstretched,
I'm combing for the bottom half.

GAPS

You're easy for me because I have a daughter, Jim said. But you can't forget how you look to us. Ex-construction-ex-loggers. Pushing sixty. You're a squirrely thing. The music you like. If you could let it be quiet on the highway. Six in the morning. We're all watching the hill-light cut off the wind turbines. We don't want to talk about our wives. It's true they should let you drive. That's why I do, but who shoveled the tires out. For you. Painted over the torn fence. Hard to take you seriously as a guy who's had a saw through his face. Watched a razor pluck stitches off his glued eye. I'm not denying this is a shit hole. It's the last one, though. Our careers. Think how easily you got here. I know you try, you scrape your little arms up. You're right. They should handle you. It goes both ways. None of it's you, really. Just you in this place.

EXHIBITS: AFTER THE DAM FLOODED
THE TOWN OF VANTAGE

I.

      with the dam came
  flood   it

      took forty hours to fill

    a twenty-mile basin   Unofficial

Mayor said   *we pried homes out &*

built town again

     on top of the   canyon

hammered nails in original
holes

      Structures hauled piece by piece up the new road

    50's diner relocated

its floor warped
aslant

      Reservoir filled what we abandoned

        algae-hooded shacks
a planked

     foundation map

II.

(We were kids dunking faces off the sides of our parents'
drift boats
eyes open)

Dad jokes

imagine sturgeon pacing the frozen aisle

sucking clams off living room
furniture   like your furniture
slime

under water

You can dive still   see

half the Spanish castle

its stone pile   a trap

Web of weighted grocery bags

III.

*What really got them after relocation
were the snakes*

Giving a tour the

woman at Vantage Museum touched
her name badge

*In the flood all the holes blew out
hundreds displaced
the rattling was
a constant sound*

What the dog brought in while you slept

Had to wear thick on your feet

until   all in a day they

pushed into ground like
no longer angry

RAY

The thing all women have is mouths,
he says in the work truck, *that don't shut.*
Let me drive once, I broke
in hot sand. Shoveling the tires loose
so much of his body spills
over his pants. Calls me princess.
Pops the hood warms his
breakfast on the engine.
These are life lessons—
how to clean trash cans:
lighter fluid and a cigarette.
All it takes to hypnotize a chicken
is its neck in your armpit.
What you need is to kill
something and eat it.
He finds old condoms
to chuck at me, hornet nests
stuck in Pepsi cans he calls
Michael Jacksons. Getting stung
is crew initiation. Bets I've never
worked a day, shows me
lumps where a saw slipped
through his face. Lets me struggle
over the dumpster:
you should have to weigh more
than this bag of garbage
for them to pay you
to throw away.

UNREPORTED INCIDENTS

Ray spit in my hand. Motor oil
        leafed on still water, and he spoke over me
saying I waver when I issue commands.

He kicked the drowned cat to shower me
        with its pocket of brown lake.
Said I wasn't worth the fuss I made

showing the boys their loneliness in the country
        where trucks sink to bone
under the blue sound of electricity.

Ray invented the game *chopstick snake*
        with two branches he tossed
a rattler at the back of my legs.

Eventually he decided it wasn't his job to help me.
        A circle of drunk men, burning
illegally. Their faces sockets of cracked light.

He laughed, *go on. Tell them*
        to call it a night. My hands were behind
my back when I asked, *could you please.*

I turned to Ray. He smiled, reversed away
        as one man crushed a can
another draped his wet arm over me.

THIS IS A TARGET

Any moment a terrorist. Why we radio the man in the tower before crossing the dam. Bright Hawaiian t-shirt, his silhouette. He nods or shakes his head. This is the field below the dam you check for power-line markers that slip off during windstorms and crack in half. You can spot them from the freeway. Orange shells big as a bathtub. When you get in one it shows you as small to the men around you. You make them laugh when they can see you, and they only see you in relation to them being the man. This is where you set the beaver trap. Staple wires at the stumps of what few trees stand. Signs you drive stop boats from loading in endangered wetlands. This is where the wind knocked the train off the bridge to the bottom of the river. Foundations of what was built around the tracks. Cinderblocks, graffiti. Your face on the screen of your phone in a blue outhouse. Boys from your high school starting a fire during the burn ban. Nobody listens specifically when you ask so you kick the rocks and a dozen mice scramble out. This is your thick uniform. Each part. Glossy line through your hair where a ponytail holder shielded dirt. When your boss starts the game of *who can find the strangest piece of trash*. Dunes where Ray hid the peg-leg before work. The meal at Olive Garden he won for bringing it back. This is the most giant American flag. Line of white trucks with numbers on the back. The job a registered sex offender had. Hot water on the hot sand. A little red knife you got from your dad.

CLEANING OUTHOUSES

I never saw them but I knew people shot our outhouses. The holes let black widows in. Once I waited an hour for one to step off a webbed door handle. Nobody helped from outside. We didn't pump the basin but cleaned surfaces like you would a regular bathroom. Speared up the trash. I remember sweeping a wad of shredded toilet paper and pulling open a litter of mice. Gravel snipped skin and they struggled back to the paper—shut eyes like people swimming, arms at their sides. I didn't feel one I caught with a broom and broke across the plastic floor. I put them back in a corner. Tore a sheet from my notebook and spoke to whoever came next like *don't* or *please* or *look before you.* A tent my blue handwriting. One of those things you wouldn't notice until you noticed, in the blend of what you'd been hearing, their crying.

ELK SPLAT

The canyon the river ran through was bowl-shaped and you could see from the water sometimes sheep on its rim. Our boat noise would collect in one wall and spill over the ledge of the next. That must've been what happened—a jet ski, for example, cutting through the middle of the gorge can sound like a gun going off—the elk caught the ricocheting of blared engine, thought it was a hunter, jumped for the river and missed. Their twenty-seven bodies formed a triangle of hide and bone. Some parts preserved under water. Half a leg or a smashed face like bees I've seen in tree sap. There was little we could do to move them. They accumulated trash—sunglasses, Dorito bags, disposable cameras—what people dropped photographing themselves next to the mess. Locals started calling it *Elk Splat*. We'd shovel through with litter grabbers, knocking maggots into the river, holding shirts halfway up our heads. Whoever'd spooked the elk was the kind of person we liked to imagine as one-rich-kid. What we were better than. Fucking rich kids slicing the reservoir in half. *Who else would kill an elk and leave the antlers.* How could you not think to freeze all those years of good meat.

HATCHERY

Grayson takes an apple & snaps it in half
with the pads of his hands over

one knee   When he throws beer glass
at the fire pit   he means to almost target me

      I'm digging my grave in the backyard
he says   *never fucking leaving this goddam*

weeds blow off stem   A little factory
carves its milky glow   he milks salmon

Oil color   dead-salmon-bin   *If we didn't have to*
if anybody knew he says sideways sliding chew

into his lip   When he spits the dirt makes
a red sack he twists   until it smears in

APPLES

I unwind a reel of company caution tape
tie it in a tight line
from the rearview mirror
to the middle seat—

severing the truck cab—my thumb nail
pried in the divot of the Buck-knife
blade at my knees.

Grayson drove us out of service,
parked in dirt between orchard trees.
Took his hands off the wheel,
turned to me.

Somewhere there, a plastic bucket
of rotting apples. Pale and soupy.
Skin slipped off, floating flat on top
like wax wrappers from candy.

(Imagine the rose deodorizer of a clean outhouse.)

Drink some, he said, I dare you.
Put one in your mouth.

GRAVE BY THE LAKE

Jim was like a dad. He told me to stay,
I jumped from the truck. Followed to a plastic
tub in the gravel lot. Its opening white
and fanned as dead leaves. Backlit,
we could see the case held a body. We gloved
our noses. It burned to breathe, like ice in your nose
or inhaling chlorine. Jim crouched beside it,
some pit mix. A pet left there meant no money
to cremate. No yard to bury in. We lifted
the tub. Hands under both sides. Top wedged
with my chin. I could see his body
had been stuffed to fit, as if placing him
in a box made up for his abandonment.
Digging a grave requires a permit.
Our company provided a dumpster
for carcasses. Half a mile from headquarters,
downwind. There was what we had to do
with the dog and what Jim knew I wanted.
He turned to me, exhaled, drove away from the dam.
We found a field without security cameras
and lugged the mutt out. Fingers cut
through grass. We dropped the box in a shallow hole.
Covered damp dirt with gravel. Projecting
what the family would have wanted,
we said a few words. Unclipped and hung nearby
his heart-shaped tag. Jim was a dad, he knew
to set a flowery weed. Those were the ways
he made work light for me. Said if someone were here
with his daughter—standing by the flat
water, old blood on her baseball hat—
he would want him to tell her not to come back.

ANGELA

This is no place Jim said. Kicked out a cigarette. Took my shoulder, pointed through a gas station at his daughter folding silverware into a napkin. She set two Styrofoam cups out—for us—on the glass. *Can't tell yet she's pregnant. Drug dealer boyfriend wrecks what I give her, there's nothing I can.* He motioned down the road. *Remember that meth lab?* I remembered intensive training. Charcoal remains. A house and our blue masks. The kind of information that was to have: notice if striking strips are torn off matchbooks, batteries drained, gloves, the odor of the ash. It was early. We drank coffee. On our way out his daughter snagged my uniform with her hand. Smiled long. Turned away from Jim's back. *Take care of my dad.* I nodded. We watched him smoke again, the grey dirt and warped railroad tracks. *Smells like hot acid,* he said when I came to stand beside him. *Her baby's going to breathe like that.*

ROAD SALVAGE

Jim made me think what it would mean to think
as a family. Our hands
scored with splinters, dismantling cabins
for the company.
He stashed a pile away from the fire we worked
slow loading.
Planning to haul it home at the end of the day,
to make a fort
for his on-the-way grandkid. The wood
was still good, just
blocking condo development. He could
sand the lead off it.
Run water through that building, give
the girl a working sink.
After finding his pile, our bosses
made Jim carry slats
to the garbage. That was stealing technically,
the old nails and paint
a liability. He came back, raided
the trash at two
in the morning. Called that impulse *bodily*.
To resist systems
that hinder providing for a family.
A husband's instinct,
for example, to swerve for the white end
of a buck hooked
around guard rails. Taking his knife out,
he asked me to brace
its neck—still hot—while he hacked into the
head. Points breaking off
with roots and a square of skin. He explained
his wife liked antlers
as weight for the paper on mornings when

it was warm enough
to open a window. He let them whiten
in the truck-bed,
forgetting a boss would see, and when one did
Jim covered for me.
Said he'd threatened me not to repeat,
that I'd sat angrily
while he dismembered the body. I didn't
know until coming
back. After they suspended him I said,
on the phone, *it's like*
when farmers slaughter and bury pigs
in Grapes of Wrath. To value
profit and insurance policies over
actual impact.
Jim laughed. *I'm not starving.* He said
if they let him on
again he'd fire me so I could read—find
a reference that
didn't cast him as some dust bowl feeding
his family from the trash.

BIOLOGICAL CONTROL TASK

We were taking lunch, sharing a crumpled
bag of Goldfish below the dam
when we met Bill and Mike.

They rolled down a window, pulled up
next to our truck and strained
their necks—looking over me
—to introduce themselves to Jim.

They have the same face when I remember them.
Two guns propped between seats,
smell from the old engine.

Tarp over a load in the bed.
What've you got? Jim asked.

They stepped out, undid a rope.
Something soft hit
dirt on the opposite side of the truck.

You might not want to look. Bill glanced at me,
slid the tarp off. The mound there
was grey and white, at first I thought
dirty laundry.

At least eighty seagulls just dead,
ropes of blood at the chests. Shot so
their shoulders folded apart
like wet book covers.

To protect salmon.
Doesn't make sense, but it's not bad
getting paid to hunt.

Mike motioned to a trash bag on the pile.
Show them our girl.

Bill drew it down, ripped the knot, lifted
an adult heron with a hole blown
out the chest.

He held both webbed feet.
You could look through her body.

*We found her in the road. Hit
by a hatchery cannon.*

The bird seemed frozen,
wrongly intact—gold eyes cranked
open, neck coiled tight over her slaty back.

When I cried it made them comfortable like I could be
a daughter, wife or something they knew how to see.
Hands on my back.

What's the matter, Mike asked. *Didn't you care
about the gulls or were they too ugly?*

WHAT THE DAM HAD TO PASS

Whenever someone didn't fit you knew it was because of a dad. A dad being someone big. Hard to get anywhere on your own especially in a place that thick. The ladder we climbed went from down in the wet tunnels of the dam up to a hole of blue light. Getting out a literal sense. Considering this system it was irritating when someone had the ability to use a dad. I needed a summer job. There were people my dad knew would answer if he called. Before the interview I sat in a State Park folding grass. The reservoir looked to me a living thing not hung with latex & beer cans. When I stepped into the stilted trailer the crew knew I was because of a dad. They taught me rules like not to put in my feet. How to steal onions from a field before work at four in the morning. That there were tests the dam had to pass. Every ten years our bosses filed for a Federal License. Sent studies of our biological impact. We were photographed prodding through spills of garbage. While rolling magnets to pry nails from sand. My dad at a desk stamped the License. My dad at a ladder counted the fish. The only way to fit was not to let anyone discuss my relationship. I earned respect through what I pretended not to see. Vodka water bottles. Grayson's hand wide on my knee. I had the privilege of going in thinking nobody could touch me.

ORCHARD, CUT OUT

The smell of Grayson's energy drink
was like a melting battery in the rain.

After all day painting stumps
I jumped out of a moving truck

because he gripped the side of my face.
A misunderstanding, he said.

And that was the thought I always had,
alone in a cab with a man: would the grass

soften the impact? The door clipped
my forehead on the way down.

Lucky for the apple field, he said
lucky you didn't pull this shit on flat ground.

He held both of my wrists and the vehicle
stalled. And the river. Here's what is

already known. The remains of the trees
were blaring. Two hundred neon globes.

You can see my right eyebrow still bends
wrong around a divot like an arrow.

THIS IS ABOUT THE DAM

Its orange bug light. Being in and outside the turbine shafts, blenders fused to bowls. The little road we used to get across. Flat waves shooting out a single fan. In the job interview I wore a dress unlike me. Tied at the back. I was introduced to a room of men. People of the dam are designed to protect you from what could happen while working. They administered hepatitis shots. Required us to pass computer tests on safety and sexual harassment. This is about the dam. When I fell out of a tree they threatened to fire me for climbing. When Park put his Happy Meal crown on my head they saw and threatened again. I was learning one thing. At the end of the summer in an empty gym cafeteria I sat with my boss's boss across a plastic table. *I'm so sorry*, he said and they un-invited Park back. This is about the dam. The loop of houses beside the dam. Smudge out one of them.

RULES

I couldn't have Park because he belonged above me—different colors of the same garbage suit—I was creative with how I communicated that I'd like to. Almost none of my feelings for him were about him. I needed to resist the line. The line represented my lack of agency. My resistance invented a third space, which challenged the rule by suggesting that rules could be manipulated without breaking. Like when we, on the job, walking across the plate-shaped rock below the dam, met a fisherman with a deep hole in his head left from brain surgery. How, after he dared us to put our fingers in, Park did because he knew I'd get something out of it—sweeping the fisherman's hair open in the back. That was touching and not touching me. Describing. Making eye contact.

OWNERSHIP

How much of Ray squatting naked in that field off the freeway
belongs to me? I was there not hearing him ask to turn back.
Radio on my belt rattling. This kind of abandoning was specific
to me: stabbing through beached flip-flops, flirting. All day a trail
cut into dry grass under the bridge. Where dumpsites collect.
We didn't speak. You slid the garbage bag from my back pocket,
shook until it punched open. These are the images I swore not
to repeat: Ray wore suspenders under his uniform, had to take
off everything. Used whatever paper stuck to the brush already.
Later, I wondered why he was quiet, shifting beside you in the
front seat. Your eyes the mirrors driving. I played a passive part
in exploiting. Even now. I make it hard for myself to blame me.

THE ROCK MAN

I knew I loved Park with fish blood on his hands. The way he smelled like fish blood & smoke. Park was my boss so we never rode in the same truck even when he loved her he loved me so I sat with Ray. Ray said things I had to look up like *nice beehive* after I put my hair in a ponytail. Or when he got upset he'd talk about *The Rock Man*, which I thought was a wrestler but is actually a character made of rocks from a cartoon narrated by Ringo Starr. *Being a rock is a very heavy life*, Ray said while we lifted bags of gutted salmon out of trashcans into the truck bed. The one time Park & I spoke on the phone he told me Ray had gone home (the night before) to find his wife dead on a La-Z-Boy in their front room. I was at the river already, coming down. Park let me in his truck. During lunch we went to Park's house by the dam with balloons, newspaper, & flour. We blew cylindrical shapes, pasting them together to form a miniature Rock Man. We meant to give this to Ray. Park said his girlfriend was moving out. Her handwriting a red sprawl across the refrigerator. We waited for the papier-mâché to dry & he smelled like glue, kissing me, putting himself in my hands. I fell out of love with him & I did that to every man. That night when we found Ray—arm-pitting a bottle of Yukon Jack—he said The Rock Man had stopped by before us. He couldn't stand so Park sat on his lap and held him. Two huge men. I slid the bottle in the freezer while Park promised The Man would come again. But we couldn't. After they fired him, Park dropped hardened balloon pieces in a compartment in the back of my truck. I knew it came from Park before I opened it; I recognized the way the fifty-gallon bag was tied at the neck. I was ten years younger than him, doing the things I did then.

That was me combing the bee legs out. My ponytail a hot nest. Wanting simple. Eating french fries from your mouth. Saying yes I would like. Series of company website photographs. Click on me posed in a tube where the horse floated out. *Washington's Palm Springs*. Please come visit you your whole family. My pulled up weedy feet. That was the purple eyeliner month. Landshark and Burnett's buried in dirt behind my parents. When I ate the most hot dogs extra large pizza lunch. How small and how much. I hiked a car door from a pasture in the summer drought. Strapped to my belt. Waved while stabbing cups off. My friends Slurpees and bikinis. Guys called them a bald eagle sighting. Added four to the tally. We were the kind they'd like to see at the nude beach but a nude beach is never what you think. Twenty-person tents. Golfer wearing a yellow dick-sling. That was when they left me to clean. A man should never see another man fucking even in the movies. Worst things work against biology. For example who would put a teenage girl this far from cell service. Problem of access. Car tires stuffed in vault toilets. My new awareness. Burying tampons in an open field. Dirt stamped my bright hands. It was funny they drove away when I pulled down my pants. I could run the two miles back and it was like me to hold the radio to my mouth. So they'd hear. I heard too from the truck speakers driving up the road. How balanced how practiced I was at that clipped breath.

RESERVOIR

Where did you meet her,
Park asked.

By the fence, the weed
whacker

she was towering her hair
fingers
teasing out dead grass.

It was her job, she
shoveled the bathroom
snakes in half.

I didn't know how.

Stained glass
at the peak of the house.
Crouched in

her attic room. Wood and wire.
Insulation
stapled with tapestries.

I put my leg between her legs.

I could.
I didn't want to be

a boy sliding

off her bra
with one hand.

First time
both ways

burning the end on a short string—

thinking
I only have a little left of
what

She cut a flower from
the yard

when she left
before me.

It's the same when anyone leaves
their handwriting.

It's the same.

She hasn't.

I feel she's done a bad thing.

When I hear your name
she said

I think
of your wrists.

This made lake.

As empty as
water gets.

VISITOR'S CENTER

I feel her loosen grip on me,
moving, fingers pressed
to cool Plexiglas.
We stare into an exposed hatchery pond,
watching as the 10-foot
sturgeon slides through a shoal
of hovering Coho,
snapping into sight with elongated
upper-tail lobes.
It's all bone plates,
smooth scutes
catching like knives
in shafts of light.
It turns to suck on the side of the tank.
Toothless mouth level
with our faces
fleshy barbels
hanging over gums.
I imagine it gnawing
on the muscular hinges
of clam shells—opening
to swallow salmon whole.
It's called thunder,
when sturgeon slap their swim
bladders to attract
each other, small sounds
reverberating in a river.
I wonder if the impulse fades here:
echoing alone in a pool of concrete—
like how could you wait, still reach after
every time you've strained,
bent your body's length
to communicate.

NEW HIRE

Real fine heifer / low class beauty / what do you call those blonde
/ feathering / got yourself a new work buddy / not the only /
Victoria's Secret / pulling plastic from the reeds / she walks like
she / begging / I'd give my / see her bend again / please / how
many colors of lace / shoe string / her strapped black / can you
imagine / bleached / I've got a family / you might be the same
/ like a different breed / poor thing you / couldn't compete /
could learn a / thank God thank affirmative action / I'm reeling
it in / calling my children / I'm a good / never cheated but / if
you wonder why she's not out / spearing / in the weeds she /
flashed the crew lead / he said he / right in truck 43 / ten out of
/ after she lifted / ballooning / can you picture / all the effort
/ of her / how does she walk with / gathering all that weight /
into her / can you imagine her / like I already know her / out
of her / clothing

INVITATION

Lowering a window, Sara lit a cigarette. *So you like girls*, she said, *but you used to do men?* She dug a stick of glitter from her purse and pressed down on my right eyelid. *I have a friend like that. She had a bad thing happen her first time at sex. Sex with men.* I nodded. My eyes ringed with purple like reversed lily pads. Sugar from a bag of gummy worms cracked in our teeth. *You could be really stunning*, she said, *like if you lived in a city.* I laughed and reached for the cigarette. *Now I have your virginity*, she winked. She told me that night she was going to be the girl at an all-guys party in Richland. *You should come.* She smiled like people smile before they break something. *Don't lie to me,* she said, holding out her phone with the image of the invitation. *Have you ever pictured yourself at the center like that, being fucked by a group of men?*

BODY COUNTING

Accustomed to our baked skin, it was hard to remember we smelled like wet garbage until we sputtered past people who fakevomitted or threw Solo cups in our wake. Like everyone working for the dam, we maintained an image of functionality. A dam is justified by its abundance in each category: power, irrigation, navigation, recreation. Every body on the water proves that its unnatural swelling has utility. For us this meant drifting uncomfortably close to recreators and counting with a loud clicker, our data demonstrating how and where the reservoir was used as a space. Flags clumped on a grey grid like ticks on deer skin.

. . .

When a dam proves purposeless the government can, theoretically, take it away. Every ten years the district files to renew their federal license, sending ours and other collected numbers to the state. On counting days we were assured our efforts meant something to commissioners personally. Sugar cookies and black coffee. The sort of things you offer someone after they donate a sack of their own blood, buy a house from you, count your bodies.

. . .

We liked to imagine what it would look like to revoke a dam. Crush it out. Expose a scattered history. We were aware of what was sacrificed for the affordability of electricity. That, when considering the common good, flooding a truck stop town meant nothing in comparison to lit-up houses, ours especially. We never understood the generation of power but that the power was sent in boxes to other states. The dam is safe due to the level at which it generates. We'd heard of abandoned buildings one hundred feet below us accumulating algae. The erasure of Wanapum land, so much land. Knowing what we knew about the reservoir it was difficult to count the people half naked and vodka drunk on a jet ski. They cut past. You could hear the water burning. To gather

floating wrappers. Check the list of boxes saying these are impor-
tant. These are the communities the dam is serving.

. . .

The dam is a line after which the river is class-divided. i.e. where
is higher up, where has less cattle-ditch run-off billowing into
it. On the south end fewer bodies, a different sense of purpose.
There we'd count families swimming in the holes where tributar-
ies met the river. Children jumping off the knobbed branches of
cottonwood trees. That was the longest stretch without a town.
Buildings abandoned after the failure of the local railroad indus-
try. People sat between cinder block foundations, digging rods
into river rock to reel in ten-foot sturgeon. These were people
who worked on the orchards, the nuclear reservation, or with us
for the dam in some capacity.

. . .

The resorts north of the dam were illegally lodged in protected
wetlands. Harsh, imported stones jutting around grey, repetitive
condo buildings. Vacation homes of kids I knew from high school.
While we counted their party barges, I twisted my recognizably
curly hair into a baseball hat. Their glowing bodies were the most
beautiful I'd ever seen, so forced tan like after peeling the first
layer of bark off a pine tree. Walking an exposed sand dune, I had
trash bags tied through my belt loops. I thought, finding bottles of
lube and whiskey in the brush, how I wanted to be someone with
no register of environmental impact. My sweating jeans. I hated
the crew for looking at the laying girls around me.

. . .

Once, we counted four hundred recreators in one stretch. Spiral-
ing footballs. Different stations of the same country music. None
of them thinking their noise as a kind of violence. The steady
motions of a deer's head as it swam, displaced, between those
thin islands.

GOOD MEN PROCESS

Grayson stood at the edge of a cherry orchard.
The bicyclist under the emergency blanket, a crumpled boulder.
Ten minutes earlier he'd radioed *help here.*
Didn't say *this is truck 80,* or, *over.*
Instead, he held the microphone to his lips, breathing
quiet, asked if we could hear sirens
from where we were. But we were nowhere.
Gathering hot trash into bags.
Always too far to meet each other, for example,
if one group saw the rare clusters
of approaching bighorn. When Grayson spotted
the hit bicyclist—I won't open that image—
the rest of us were twenty miles north.
We registered, even in our panic, the level
at which he controlled his reaction. I wanted to ask
what happened, but Jim and Ray refused,
as good men, they respected Grayson's silence.
Good men holding the radio up between them
in the front seat. Forgetting the blinker
was running. The classic-rock static loud
as we pulled from Douglas County,
chasing the occasional sound of him.
We listened, like being there with Grayson
for all the minutes it took an ambulance to haul
over plates of boiling asphalt.
After reporting the incident,
Grayson locked himself in a work trailer.
The fire-season moon combed red into the desert.
We waited against the hoods of our rigs.
Good in that we swore none would leave without him.
Good because we surrendered pride,
saying we hoped he cried then. Shaking our heads
at all he had to stomach. And, come

bug noise, night wind, and a scared call
from Jim's oldest-young kid,
they turned to me. Said, reluctantly,
as if it was too much to trust me with,
that I was the only one small, the only one sensitive.
After I agreed, they wedged a screen from a window
and offered their joined hands as steps
for me to climb in. I twisted through the frame.
Fell next to Grayson, who grasped
a bottle of hand sanitizer like a weapon.
I remembered then how afraid I was of him.
The oil on his face lamp-lit.
The crying gathered at his chin.
I saw him like I'd never seen a man,
digging his forehead into the bones
of my chest. *I haven't hugged a woman in years,*
he said. *I didn't know we had that much blood in our heads.*
I smelled sanitizer on his undershirt,
saw where red sifted brown through his uniform.
The creases of his fingers cleared from scrubbing.
He didn't have to say, it was obvious the parts of his body
that had made contact, holding together
the pieces of that man. I scoured each drawer and closet,
not knowing what to look for.
Finding a bag of Fourth-of-July balloons,
I sat back on the floor. Blew into one
while he stared from his corner.
I sensed he was rooted there, like I'd known the bicyclist
was dead the moment we parked.
How Jim and Ray pushed me into the seat.
Jim saying: *don't make this about you, I can't*

get you through this. I felt too much a kid and woman.
Watching fire trucks through a muddy window.

In the trailer, I tied the balloon and put it at Grayson's hip.
He glanced at it. I filled the rest
until I'd given the room my breath.
He punched the balloons off his lap. Laughed
at the hair reaching in vertical wires off my head.
Laughed too hard like dropping dishes.
Don't let them hit the floor. He said. Beating them.
I ran around the room with my hands.
I would have done anything; I knew what it meant
for him to see them just-miss the carpet.
And that's what the crew said when I came out
with him on my shoulder.
Ray, for the first time, keeping my glance.
He compressed Grayson's enormous body like a blanket.
Jesus Christ. Jim said. *What a summer we've had.*
His fist an opening ball on my back. What a long stretch
of nobody seeing what his others were good at.

ELK TOOTH NECKLACE

The first time Ray lost a wife he didn't know why.
At work he thumbed a scar on his forehead
to show us where she'd split skin with a water glass—
the bitch—he said the kids, by moving
to Alaska, took her side. The baseboard lined
with spent whiskey bottles. He'd walk barefoot
in the snow. He sheeted the porch in plastic
so that the house resembled itself,
a stonefly rising from its molt. Around
that time, elk took to staring through living
room windows. Their yellow eyes pulsed in sports light,
hanging, ghostly, among hollow trees.
Once, he dove at them hollering like you would spook
a group of crows. *That's the gist of it,*
he explained on lunch break. He didn't know how
he stumbled into the Teanaway
Wilderness or what became of his clothes. He woke
facing an elk's bullet-torn throat. Smiling
while eating in a circle around his truck, we found
the story hard to believe. He'd only
caved and offered up that much after months of us
calling him gay, a handful of women's
names for the necklace he kept under his work polo:
a wooden corn nut latched to a silver chain.
Ray claimed he'd gone back, sober, the next day
and worked the tooth from the elk's hard mouth.
You should've seen the rack. He held out his hands.
Two saplings. *I could've froze to death,*
he said, *just think, drunk off my ass, I killed that thing.*

The second time, he came home to find Darla
cold at the TV. It was embarrassing.
We didn't know him when he sobbed his face

into a crust and kicked out the door screen.
A neighbor cooked apple pie and roast beef. We fed
him, took turns lifting the fork, letting him
drink. Nobody else called or knocked. We, the garbage
crew, were his only company. That morning
he asked us to leave. Lifted the chain from his neck
and handed it to me. When he said
I want you all to have it, but it's got magic
you can't understand, I thought he meant
how it feels to save your own life by taking warmth
from another body. The strength of having
felt yourself bend. For the rest of the season,
none of us spoke of his absence. We never
went again. I hung the chain from the rearview mirror
where it swung between our heads. We imagined
Ray would die, and every day we waited
we felt we made it happen.

On the last shift we passed a cigar between us,
a ceremony for the final bag of trash.
We shut our doors, drove off in the same moment.
Dirt shrouded the boxcar where we'd kept
our things. While turning I saw the necklace, its chain
catching light in the cab of truck 43.
I dug through my pockets and remembered
that we'd surrendered our keys. If they hadn't
yet the guys would soon realize. Five cars taking
the highway through the canyon. Their blocked
music. I pictured them silently weighing
the consequences of going back for
the necklace, breaking in. Crossing the bridge
over the gate where the river opens
at 5:oopm. Heading home, we used to stop there,
above the water, and though the fall is too slow
to see, we'd squint long enough to convince ourselves
we were the reason the reservoir emptied.

DRINKING IN THE COMPANY TRUCK

We're six, tossing glass beer bottles
at the hole of a fire pit. Six worn-through

back pockets. The print of chew-disks. We spit
red. We smoke. Binocular women

on speed boats. Call their chests bald eagles.
Jail bait. Joke about one's daughter's age. Six

experience labor devaluation—
ex-loggers ex-construction. Six thieves

in a field of onions. Cry while skins open.
The freeway heat. Cry drinking water

bottle whiskey. Corona from an empty
Pepsi. We're six hated. Six sexist.

Six reactions to one's dying wife.
The wind chimes she cut from cans of Bud Light.

How, without one, five fight. Knuckles twisted white.
Five sweep webs off the ceiling slats

of a duck blind. We're flashlights scouring that dirt
road looking for one's lost pocket knife.

LANDSCAPE, COMPARISON

When the dam cracked I
stood beside it
     isn't just the dam

I said

       friend in the gas station
     rolling change

milk jug

donations
for his cancer treatment

               Nobody came when the river left

That's a real thing the

beaten down buildings   glint

     of cars driven off a cliff

   . . .

After losing water access

      farm animal abandonment

           garbage bag body bags   rock wrapped and split

Local pawner digs up
an arrowhead   brought to examine in
          his wet fist

To make a few grand   questions of property not considering
              human displacement
                  histories of   Resorts stretched

river a balled thread

like placing different issues beside each other
in a sentence

      What is given similar weight conflates   and how a space lays out
                           its violence

STURGEON

The waiting room of the Public Utility District's office was a trophy case. Framed articles documenting the positive effects of the dams hung neatly around a massive fish tank. Images, for example, of the reservoir fostering summer communities; a family at a barbeque, grilling salmon meat. Other photos insisted on the district's commitment to environmental awareness and advocacy. There was one of my maintenance crew as we strung a wire fence around the base of the single tree that harbored a bald eagle family. When you entered the office, the fish were the first thing you saw. Their movement reminded me of wind-up toys as they bobbed from the pebbles to the surface or floated dumbly in place. Passing time between meetings, I would cool my hands on the glass. Once, the woman at the front desk asked me if I knew why the water was kept just above freezing. When I said I did not, she explained that it stunts their growth indefinitely. *So they can stay longer in the tank.* I turned to watch them. Shark figurines, following my finger with crazed, stamped-in eyes.

. . .

The gold nameplate on the tank read: *White Sturgeon, Our Fossil Fish.* Ours because they live in the river and we control its movement. Sturgeon haven't evolved in over seventy million years. Instead of scales their sides notch with triangular bone plates called scutes. Like if our spines sat on the outside of our skin. The largest sturgeon on record grew to twenty feet long and over a thousand pounds. Some live to one hundred years old. This means that sturgeon alive today experienced the building of the reservoirs. They swam the river before it stopped and were once anadromous, or accustomed to migrating between freshwater and ocean before their route was landlocked.

. . .

Dams shut off the majority of sturgeon reproduction. In stagnant water, their loose eggs coat with sand. Even if they could reproduce, it's rare they find a mate. *Sturgeon Thunder* is the term used for their attempts to call out to one another with the small noises they make by slapping themselves with their tail fins. Imagine that body sound competing against clustered party barges and racing jet skis on the surface of those reservoirs which, in some places, reach an unnatural depth of one hundred and twenty feet. As a child I swam to the bottom of swimming pools. Opening my mouth to let out air, I'd imagine myself as one of the leaves dragged to the deep. I remember listening to my mother above, how her calm voice changed shape, somehow registered as a scream.

. . .

As an employee of the PUD, I met sturgeon fishermen who made it to the windy hill below the dam every Saturday at six in the morning, where we worked picking up trash. They were rough, unshaven, and disinterested as the crew and I walked past. Once, I watched as a man laid his body on a flapping, whale-like fish until it steadied so his partner could shoot it. For these people, catching a sturgeon was as significant a win as bagging an elk with a full rack. It was like buying a whole cow: a freezer full of meat. Reeling one in could take hours. People who do so off-shore have to anchor their poles in flat river rock to keep themselves from falling. Our crew became friends with one fisherman in particular, a man named Red, who described sturgeon fishing as a matter of mental endurance and respect.

. . .

As kids swimming in the reservoir during the summer, my friends and I felt unsettled picturing these gargantuan creatures knifing through the water below our bare feet. We'd pinch each other. Make noises like swallowing. One morning while we emptied trash cans at the river, Red told our crew that when he'd had to take a month off of fishing to get brain surgery, the scariest thing was not knowing how long it would be before he could see the silver of a sturgeon on his line, pulling under the surface. In the hospital that image in his head worked as a kind of beckoning.

. . .

My father and I fought throughout my childhood with the persistent aggression that only exists between two people who refuse to surrender the shape of their memories. At different points in our lives, we both worked for these dams: me gathering trash around them, and him researching ways to improve fish passage. He currently serves as a fish biologist in Eastern Washington. He informs me that sports fishermen are some of the only advocates for funding white sturgeon restoration. *It's an ugly fish*, he says, *it's difficult to elicit empathy for them.*

. . .

Fish ladders were engineered to pass salmonids. Sturgeon are often trapped in turbine shafts, looking for a way through. While working for the dam my father rescued sturgeon by lifting them up from the lower chambers on hospital stretchers, carrying them through the narrow hallways and stairwells of the dam, and dumping them back into the reservoir. I like imagining him, at my age, executing this process: inventing a layered solution that suggested what was simple and human in every crisis.

. . .

Because they hover in the dark, spongey base of the river, sucking on clams and other crustaceans, sturgeon are easy to forget. Maybe they seem healthy because they're enormous. North American White Sturgeon are an endangered species. Recently, the district was forced to act on behalf of sturgeon through their Federal License Requirement, a process they endure every ten years to demonstrate their attempts to mitigate the environmental degradation caused by the dams. The license asked for an initiative to increase sturgeon population. This was something I could discuss with my dad. Over the phone, around a subject, my admiration for him was as acute and undisturbed as it got. He told me that the company responded to the government's demands without actually improving sturgeon habitat. Instead, they created a six-by-six spawning matrix in tanks, and after generating 6,200 offspring, the company invited locals down to the river for the release. I found a newspaper clipping of a human chain, passing the first, symbolic bucket of juvenile sturgeon to dump into the hot reservoir lake.

. . .

There is a wheel in my father's office desk that broke off the bottom of a couch in our living room after he attempted to throw it. I remember, but my sister doesn't. I covered her face with my hands. When I visit him at work to discuss my research about the dam, I talk to him across this surface. I know that the wheel is somewhere in the desk drawer above his feet. I know because he showed it to me and said that he takes it out often and decides, every time, to put it back. Some of this I understand.

. . .

On a road trip three years ago, my ex-girlfriend and I stopped the car so we could finish a fight. There we found a Visitor's Center with a sturgeon viewing tank inside. To get to it, we walked through a line of concrete hatchery ponds where thousands of trout smolt shimmered like folds of tinfoil in the direct sunlight. The viewing room was a concrete tube that looked into a pond of adult sturgeon. The fish lifelessly circled the small space. Like the plastic, worn horses of a carousel, they had a course and a set pace. My girlfriend and I stood there silently, while family after family asked us if we wanted our pictures taken with the fish, their gray bodies sliding against the glass of the tank. Claustrophobic, we forgot our fight. Instead, we thought about that kind of violence that commodifies its own impact, makes a little zoo for what it forces out of life.

. . .

Before he was like this what was he? I wonder as my father snaps at my mother in the passenger seat. I credit so much to my own inaction, to our collective inability to speak. When my sister and I were younger we'd go with our mother to his office at Fish and

Wildlife where he often housed live animals that, before they were relocated, had threatened park sites. Our favorite animal was a juvenile brown bear that sat in a chain-link cage by our father's desk: growling, sweating a foresty stink. When big horned sheep couldn't cross the freeway he hung nets from a helicopter and lifted them to safety. He is largely credited for the designation of the Hanford Reach, a wildlife preserve that protects the land poisoned by the plutonium involved in the creation of the nuclear bomb. I remember when he was flown to Washington D.C. to receive an award for his work protecting that habitat. People started calling him strong. They said he was good at pushing a message. After a government agency recruited him, he was set in a tiny office above a radio shack. He looks enormous behind a desk. His hands like baseball mitts writing documents, approving funding. He'd never cared about having political influence. He missed seeing change take physical shape, bringing my sister and I to where beavers caused pools to come back to otherwise drying streams.

. . .

When I was fourteen I met a boy who was leaving our small town to attend a Seattle university. My parents fought over how to contain our relationship. This was when my father switched. His gentleness coated in a kind of anger that seemed constant. Everything I did was in spite of him. I skipped school to meet the college boy halfway across the state. We slept in the woods in the back seats of cars in abandoned buildings in the grass beside an old winery. I felt too young to have sex so I refused his repeated advances. To me our relationship was no more than a way to redefine power, in it I thought I could find a fragment of agency.

. . .

In a borrowed sedan he said: *don't worry, this will be the fastest thing. Stay where you are. You could be asleep.*

I was shown my own nothing. Rocks cracking off the lip of a canal dam. The punch of freeway signs in car light. My own hair detached, dented like a nest in the palm of my hand.

. . .

After, hospital visits. A paper bag at my mouth. Butterfly stitches. My father carried me in. I thought I'd developed asthma or the inability to sit in tight spaces. He and my mother held what happened to me between them as a kind of evidence. What was broken? They said everything they shouldn't have: how I got myself into this situation. My father thought I couldn't be with men because of him. Maybe, he imagined, you're dating women because I was bad. *All I had to do was keep you from exactly what happened.*

. . .

When I tell people about my experience working on the maintenance crew around the dam a question some ask is, *Why would you stay?* The question tells me so much about the person who asks it. Of course I had no money and this was as well-off as I'd ever been, making overtime pulling goat heads out of trails, painting graffitied rocks grey again. But also it was the challenge. I was the only person asked in our interviews to show that I could lift 50 pounds above my head. Every day, dumping garbage, I carried more weight. To prove I could I ate ten hot dogs one lunch break. For the first time in years I felt like I operated my body. At the end of the day my parents would wait to hear my stories. They were horrified by how I carried the stench of trash, the dead animals we saw, the sexism, but they were proud of how I handled that group of men. My father and I became closer because we were some of the only people in the world thinking about the well-being of Columbia River sturgeon. How they carry history. I don't know that I would have found him again, over the weight, over the quiet, over the inability to forgive ourselves for interfering.

. . .

When we build a dam we stop flow, creating shelves of inhospitable clay. The water experiences steep temperature change. We

lose insects. The red or black streaks of healthy eggs. To restore sturgeon populations people have brought in gravel. Regraded banks. Shoveled out pools where fish can rest their overheated bodies on their way to a safer space. Even in our best attempts at reparation we excavate. Make the river like we'd shape a driveway.
. . .

There were spiders on the water the night I had to decide what I could live with. Mosquitos in the orange damlight, drumming. I wanted to stay afraid, hold to that swollenness like a moss in my neck. How could we drill down those walls of concrete. Towers drawing power from boxes. The houses the houses the houses at the edge of the made beach. We can only save the river with our memory of what the river means.

HORSE STANDS WHILE IT SLEEPS

I want to tell this without two dumpsters
                              bug line hanging at
a concrete chute

phased hands & car window   blue crust
    lettuce, tobacco smell

        of dirt in the console   I don't go

anywhere unless ways out glow

between houses

                an electric fence   in the field
the sense that what you can't see knows
to fan around

heat
        pullulating rope

        like waiting for what did to do again
again bags & that

we tied them at the neck

ACKNOWLEDGMENTS

Poems from this collection appeared in a chapbook, *Reservoir*, selected by Ocean Vuong for the 2017 *Yemassee* Chapbook Prize.

The Academy of American Poets: "Reservoir"

The American Poetry Review: "Elk Tooth Necklace" and
  "Unreported Incidents"

Blackbird: "Angela," "Grave by the Lake," and "Road Salvage"

Booth 2018 Nonfiction Prize: "Sturgeon"

Crab Creek Review: "Ray"

Cutbank Online: "Biological Control Task"

Entropy: "Body Counting"

Hayden's Ferry Review: "Elk Splat"

Hobart: "Field Guide" and "Cleaning Outhouses"

Missouri Review Online: "Orchard, Cut Out"

Narrative Magazine: "Exhibits: When the Dam Flooded
  the Town of Vantage"

The Nashville Review: "Litter" and "Visitors' Center"

New Delta Review: "The Rock Man" and "This Is About the Dam"

Passages North: "Apples"

PEN Poetry Series: "New Hire" and "Invitation"

Pleiades: "Drinking in the Company Truck"

Potluck Magazine: "Rules," "Ownership," "What the Dam Had
  to Pass," and "Horse Stands While It Sleeps"

The Southeast Review: "Good Men Process" and "Hatchery"

Timber: "This Is a Target"

This book is for my family, especially my father, Dale Bambrick. It is also for the places in rural eastern Washington that it sets out to describe, challenge, and protect.

Thank you to my friends, without whom this collection would not exist as it is. A special thank you to: Jenny Molberg, Jos Charles, Maya Zeller, Dorothy Chan, Sebastian Hasani Páramo, Colby Cotton, Jessica Lee, Danny Duffy, Kathy Whitcomb, Seanse Ducken, Lauren Loftis, Claire Meuschke, Benjamin Schaefer, Deb Gravina, Hieu Minh Nguyen, Liam Swanson, and Jenny Xu.

To the Lands and Recreation Crew, especially Ansel.

I am indebted to the conferences that supported me throughout the five-year process of writing this collection: The Bread Loaf Environmental Writers' Conference, The Bread Loaf Writers' Conference, and the Sewanee Writers' Conference. A special thank you the Bread Loaf Waiter crew of 2018.

To my most important advisor, Bruce Beasley, I am indescribably grateful. Thank you for sensing a book after reading the first poem in this collection, "Litter," and for encouraging me to see this project through.

Thank you to all of my teachers: Amber Flora Thomas, Nicole Sealey, Daisy Fried, Susan Briante, Farid Matuk, Mary Cornish, Carol Guess, Kami Westhoff, Sydney Wade, and Maurice Manning.

Thank you to Michael Wiegers, Elaina Ellis, Elizabeth Scanlon, and everyone else involved with *The American Poetry Review* and Copper Canyon Press. Working with you all on this has been a dream.

To Eavan Boland and everyone at the Wallace Stegner Fellowship at Stanford University, thank you for this time, energy, and support. I am especially grateful to Christina Ablaza, Ose Jackson, and my cohort: Colby Cotton, sam sax, Monica Sok, and Jay Deshpande.

To G, all of my love.

Thank you, Sharon Olds, for selecting this collection, for your work, for all the poems in here that you inspired.